Verse Vote

Verse Vote

Poems by
Jack Swansen

Drawings by
Julie Garcia Shea

For Virginia Garcia

ACKNOWLEDGMENTS

"Verse Curse," "No Openings," "Stunning Pouch," and "Wrong Number" first appeared in *Good Reading*; "Cold Comfort," "Husband's Fate," and "Waist Space" first appeared in *Sunshine Magazine*; "As Told To..." and "Rejected" first appeared in *Right Here;* "Fit to be Tied" first appeared in *Pepper...and Salt*; "Judgment Day" first appeared in *Mature Living*, March 1980, © Copyright 1980 The Sunday School Board of the Southern Baptist Convention. All rights reserved. Used by permission of the author.

PRINTED IN THE UNITED STATES OF AMERICA

LIBRARY OF CONGRESS CATALOGING-IN-PUBLICATION DATA
Swansen, Jack, 1909-
Verse vote : poems / Jack Swansen
ISBN 0-931832-82-9
I. Title
PS3569.W265V47 1991
811' .54--dc20 91-160
CIP

PUBLISHED BY FITHIAN PRESS
POST OFFICE BOX 1525
SANTA BARBARA, CALIFORNIA, 93102

CONTENTS

THE HAPPY HEARTH

THE BODY BEAUTIFUL

DAY IN AND DAY OUT

OUT TO PASTURE

In TV hidden-camera ads,
So unrehearsed, offhand,
Where do they go, benighted souls,
Who pick the "other" brand?

TV FARE BREAK

With those bulletins so pressing
It would be a fresh reversal
If for once they interrupted
Not the program, the commercial.

NON-SENSE

Round numbers now are in decline;
Their fall is quite intense.
Nine ninety-nine, point, ninety-nine
Lacks common dollar cents.

OTHER $_____

Caught by that devil, Mailing List,
Our correspondence awes us;
Addressed by name, we're mint-fresh grist
For untold novel causes.

INVESTMENT CLUB

From the moment of its beginning, with thoughts of
heavy winning,
We made some awful gaffes.
Many stock were bought at peaks, then took a
downward slide.
We seek market tips as each day goes, scan many
P/E ratios,
And study countless graphs.
Yet we're locked in downside drift—not much to
view with pride.
We each make a monthly deposit,
But somehow we don't do very well.
So we search for factors that must cause it.
Is it S-E-C, F-E-D, G-N-P, they or we, who can tell?
Yes, the matter of our investing is past the point of jesting.
Oooh! the ones we didn't buy!
Quietly we're looking for some help more qualified.

FORTRESS

Our inner world of tooth and gum
At times will lodge a wayward crumb,
And almost no amount of force'll
Clear that world of such wedged morsel.

SNAP JUDGMENT

I'm inclined to be most wary
When that photographic buff,
After trips quite legendary
Wants to show us all his stuff.
For his lengthy commentary
On each slide the going's rough—
I become quite arbitrary,
Want to shout, "Enough's enough!"

LEFT OUT

Surprising—the opinion poll—
In what it does foretell.
I ask, through its remote control
How can it do so well?

As base for my begrudging praise
It takes but one example:
I've never been in all my days
Part of a random sample.

ABANDONED

I can recall when life was fairly certain;
When change came slowly, and with customs firm.
Recently this pattern's been neglected.
This new dimension really makes me squirm.
Bygone days now look mighty strange.
We were all so certain those days would never change.
Now we've junk bonds, fast food, traffic overflow.
It's sad, friends, but where's our status quo?
The more things change, the more things stay the same??
The guy who thought up that one should hang his
head in shame.
Life's now one big build-up where gimmicks,
cashbacks glow.
I'd much rather have our status quo.
Reduced to digits we're filed away now on some
memory chip,
Coded down to street, town, state and zip.
The avant-garde all must "do their things" with
independent flair,
Which are mostly—to be fair—a delusion and a snare.
Robots, instant replay, electronic toys,
More and more commercials one less and less enjoys.
No matter how you slice it, or just what dice you throw,
We've lost it, sad to say, our status quo.

ARTS—NATURE—TRAVEL

TYMPANIC ALLEY

Old symphony concerts were usually themed
By tunes both baroque and romantic.
During such programs the music just streamed;
Pleased hearers both plain and pedantic.
Now music is written for cymbals, or drum,
And classicists find it nonplussing.
After a concert, with no themes to hum,
They probably leave just percussing.

MUSIC FISH STORY

A long variation beyond any doubt
Is in Schubert's quintet, often labeled "The Trout."
While granting the genius with which he planned it,
It seems each recasting takes more time to land it.

NOT AGAIN

Variations on a Theme
Sometimes get out of hand.
Composers often start on them
And promptly loose command.
Although it is a tour de force,
It's what I can't condone.
Stick with the one good Theme and just
Leave well enough alone.

SYMPHONY HA
TONIGHT
VARIATIONS ON A THEME
...uh..
WITH
TIMPANI
Shea

ONE TOO MANY

Yes, I like the great composers,
But I ache to find disposers
Who could quell most Variations on a Theme.
When the genius once has started
On his course—I'm sure uncharted—
Variations issue forth, an endless stream.

When caught up without a warning
In his tiresome re-adorning,
Which in later stages leaves me more than bored,
I'll latch on to any action
Guaranteeing any real distraction
Till his sanity can somehow be restored.

As I grudgingly endure him—
Wondering what but time can cure him—
For with one more varied run-through I'll explode;
Praying, more than apprehending,
That his orgy's reached its ending,
If he doesn't up and "have one for the road!"

FIRST THINGS FIRST

Those How-To books, I'm told, can bring
New outlets filled with fun.
But one I crave beyond all else
Is How-To-Find-Square-One.

QUEST JEST

Reluctantly we learn to face
Those snags found in a reference book;
We've localized the proper place
Which only states where else to look.

VERSE CURSE

Rhyming of "wind" with a word such as "kind"
Is something to which I am not yet resigned.
Ditto for "been" when it's coupled with "seen";
While meter is sound, elocution's not clean.
Terminal consonance one should attain,
Yet rhymists fall down on this, time and again.

ALAS, POOR BARD

Though now we tell it "like it is,"
Perhaps it's time to strike it.
Will Shakespeare's thing, whose plight it is,
Might end up "Like You Like It."

AS TOLD TO...

Today's indiscretions,
Revealed, could prove stellar;
With agent and published,
Who knows?...a best seller.

REJECTED

My writing urge, again unloosed,
I mail out verse that I've produced.
I dream they're sold. I get a boost.
Wake up! Again they're home to roost.

COLD COMFORT

Making plan for winter weather
We need prophecy that's firm.
Some say, "You should trust the colors
Of the lowly woolyworm."

How much dark at ends or middle
Is the secret of his fame;
Yet each fall I've never found two
Color-patterned just the same.

STILL LIFE

Environmental probing
In all fields is so complete,
Don't be surprised in learning
It's not safe to breathe or eat.

OUT OF SIGHT

In seeking other energy
Replacing oil and coal,
A stand of rugged windmills would,
We think, help fill that role.
Yet some might claim they spoil the view,
And say they were unsound:
They should, like most utilities,
Be buried underground.

IN DRYDOCK

I love that kind of travel ad
With surf and miles of sand,
And also youth, bikini-clad,
Disporting hand in hand.

For me it's a nostalgic lure;
I sense affairs have changed.
At best, my figure's now "mature,"
And poorly rearranged.

So when I venture to the shore
My dress is less revealing;
And sedentary, futhermore's
The range of my free-wheeling.

PEARLY STRAITS

I've been deliberating what
To say if I'm ascendant:
Confess to Pete what life hath wrought,
Or plead the 5th Amendment.

LA BELLE FRANCE

For months we talked of a trip we had planned.
Studied brochures, expenses, how all could be manned.
Friends advised us and warned us, left no stone unturned,
As to pitfalls most likely we'd not yet discerned.
Now we're through, so to you, what is due,
Is our thoughtful, in-depth trip review.

La belle France we have seen end to end.
On its beauties, yes, you can depend.
Hills both charming and steep,
Filled with vineyards and sheep;
And the cuisine encountered induced early sleep.
As to lodgings we planned day by day.
And we found them, oh what shall I say?
Towel, soap, bath? What about it? Some of that,
did without it.
But we never lacked for a bidet!
We found most inns becoming, some lacking full plumbing,
But we never lacked for our bidet.

We motored not by main route, but "shunway."
Mostly good; now and then déformée.
City streets? A debacle? Corkscrew lanes that we tackle
To inspect some chateau of an earlier siécle.
But we welcomed the end of the day,
And that challenge of just where to stay.
Now in full view, now shrouded, center stage or
damn crowded,
There it stood, ever-present bidet!

In our fast-changing mad age it is almost an adage:
La belle France seems to need—je ne sais!

THE HAPPY HEARTH

WASTE WONDER

The kitchen trash basket kept under the sink
Possesses an unexplained pull;
Though seemingly no one goes near it for hours,
Mirabile dictu! It's full.

NO OPENINGS

"Easy to open," or "Press gently here,"
"Pull up," or "Tuck tab in slot."
Everyone does these with greatest of ease,
But when I try them, it's not.

POSTAL TEASE

The envelope's stamped "Personal"
It must be something stellar!
Once opened, though, suspense is dashed
By "Dear Apartment Dweller."

OVERSAFE

Child-proof bottles for our pills
We guard against child use;
But they're so safety-engineered,
Most folks can't pry them loose.

PAST SENSE

A fact I'm unable to hide,
And one I reluctantly face,
Is: usually items I've hopelessly lost
Turn up in a logical place.

CHILD'S PLAY

A parent giving costly toys
To tots who can, among their ploys,
Reduce with ease all things to shambles,
Gambles.

LIMITED ENGAGEMENT

We really enjoy hearing grandchildren chatter;
Are pleased when tots come for a stay.
And also, in time, what we love is the patter
Of little feet going away.

TIME OUT

My eager excursions to gardens of fame
Are defeating—and no cause for laughter.
I seem to be jinxed for, like clockwork, arrive
Well before their high peaks, or just after.

Shea

PIPE DREAM

Those who smoked a pipe so demonstrably
Were the lucky type: never fidgety,
At ease, pensive. Just the kind of guy I'd like to be.
When they struck a pose, this is what I saw:
Keen eyes, goodness knows! and a strong, firm jaw.
Steady "eddies," knowing they're without a flaw.
Cool, crisp, their profiles suggesting they had nerves steel.
But I must pause to tell you just how I feel.

The pipe smokers I see, meerschaum or brier,
Merely inspire excessive ire.
They always need "one more match."
And they lose composure when they've, I'll vouch,
Mislaid their pouch. Absolute grouch!
I overlook all that—natch!
With old penknife they like as not'll start
scraping out dottle,
Some of which the ashtrays may catch.
Followed closely by la creme de la creme:
Just picture them, reaming the stem,
To start once more—"got a match?"

STUNNING POUCH

Her handbag's so dainty
I can't help but say,
"It might hold her key ring,
A comb, perfume spray...."
Yet forced in a crisis
It seems that she brings
From its small recesses
Innumerable things!

IT'S THE TRUCE

My wife's not pushing ERA—
Defers to me, gives me my head.
She's right, but there's that nagging hunch
That like as not I'm being led.

HUSBAND'S FATE

Going shopping it's my theory
(And it isn't only mine)
That my wife's list's all-inclusive,
Till we reach the check-out line.
As I hand up all the foodstuffs
And the clerk records each sale,
It's uncanny! she's gone back for
One more item—without fail!

JUDGMENT DAY

One task I'm not cut out to do
Is shopping for my wife.
In supermarts decisions can
Take years right off your life.

My mate agrees the past confirms
My record's not the best;
It's only as a last resort
I'm sent on any quest.

A crisis comes, the time is short,
Ingredients are lacking.
She briefs me with a small food list,
And storeward I'm sent packing.

Unhappily, one risk still looms
For which there's no defense:
Her parting words, "Dear, if they're out,
Just use your common sense."

WRONG NUMBER

His wife keeps in touch by long distance.
Her questions leave no stone unturned.
Any news there might be she uncovers—
A knack for him still to be learned.

She complains he should help with her phoning,
And by fiat he makes the next call.
Yet she knows when he lifts the receiver
He is apt not to function at all.

Off he goes very much like a martyr
Who's resigned to the fate of this task.
When returning with word of his phoning
He's confronted with "But did you ask...?"

LOVELY TIME

I'm to meet my wife in there,
But even outside hear the blare—
A bash put on by people name of Bly.
It's a big one, cars galore,
See them streaming through the door!
If left to me it's one that I'd pass by;
But on this, we don't see eye to eye....

I always get confused at large parties,
Especially when left on my own.
"Why no, we haven't met, m'am,
You see I'm Jack, not Chet, m'am."
It's things like this to which I seem prone.
I'm dead if I don't talk to the hostess,
But milling through this crush is a strain.
There she is! "Oh, Mrs. Bly,
Want to say my wife and I...."
I stopped. She had a look of pain.
Then she patted me and said, "I'm Anne Williams.
The Blys live on the *next* lane."

HANG UP

If I'm free, the phone is silent;
If tied up, it's bound to ring;
When away from it some distance,
It can't wait to do its thing.
Sure each time if left unanswered
It's the call to change my lot—
Knowing better, can I merely
Let it ring? No, I cannot.

TURNABOUT

I stole this moment to sit down and rest.
With duties switched I often feel depressed.
New chores unsettle me.
Where will it end? Just have to wait and see.
We're in transition, going every which way.
Things are in a mess.
I mind the store, and she's out every day!
Man, I'm under stress!

It's those new refinements in today's lifestyle.
But I'm not convinced that they've all proved worthwhile.
The gender gap's grown thinner;
We've had switches in breadwinner;
Someone *else* now gets the dinner—
See what I mean?
She's "careering." I'm back home, I cook, I shop,
Do the laundry, clean the house from base to top;
Bedroom, bathroom, hall and kitchen—
I'm the guy who's in there pitchin'!
Don't forget as we support them all we can,
Back of each successful gal—you'll find a man!

RAPPORT

Long years before, we'd built up rapport,
And soon half-spoken words were all we'd need to use.
My talk's still clear, but hers? Oh dear!
Haphazard thoughts are cast adrift.
They do confuse—and trouble brews....

Said today she talked to Mabel. Mabel who?
Jones, or Webb, or Gray?
While I used to link without surnames these various dames,
Rapport has gone astray.
Now I have to listen closer, for at times the
keyword's just left out.
So I ask, "Are you addressing me?" It well could be
She's talking to herself. This uncertainty is my quandary.
Then at times we'll be conversing inside, outside, anywhere.
If our contact falters, she's bound to declare,
"Speak up, dear, and stop your mumbling!"
What I bear!
Then that *other* vexing problem: When she
talks and also walks *away!*
I reply though she is out of sight, my voice pitched right.
For instance, like today.
First she asks me my opinion. Then away!
Some distant household chore.
While it called for a complex reply, at least I'd try
To pop back in the groove, and to verify
rapport was still high.
My reply *was* quite lengthy, and I strained my voice, it's true.
Didn't see her note till *finally* I was through.
It said, "Gone to *Mabel's*—back in an hour or two."

THE BODY BEAUTIFUL

TOPPING OUT

Short hairstyle's out. An ample thatch
Sets off the well groomed man.
On us it's tough who only grow
It where (and if) we can.

NO WEIGH!

Dieting's
Disquieting,
But indulging's
Bulging.

WAIST SPACE

The tailor measured me for slacks—
Asked what my waist might be
I pulled it in, said, "Thirty-nine."
"You're right," he beamed, "plus three."

NO BRUMMELL

Ads that feature manikins
In upscale sportswear clothes
Hint life can be one endless joy—
It's not, as goodness knows.
For when I try on garb like theirs,
The mirror gives no boost.
The nugget to be gleaned from this
Is: Up, it seems, I can't be spruced.

TOO CLEAR

We all revere the open mind.
For years I did pursue it.
Beyond all hopes I've had success—
My thoughts now zip right through it.

FIT SOLUTION

I jog, I train, test every diet.
Yes, each new fad, I've had to try it.
But nothing works. The one thing left?
Some tailor who's extremely deft.

FIT TO BE TIED

When young I was athletic—
A fact now best forgot.
Although my spirit's willing,
I find my muscles knot.

CHANGE OF PACE

We've reached an age, and it's reminiscent
What life now isn't for us.
It used to be so active,
So easy, with no strain or fuss.
But as we add years to our frame
We must realize things are not the same.
While approaching so-called maturity,
Wondering which aspects give security—
Comes a change of pace, and what we'd like to know:
Must pleasures now be limited, vicarious?
Our interests hold—well, not so bold.
We still express rapture, but now need a nap. Sure
It's our frame of mind that must be realigned
To a less frenetic race.
Press forward. Above all, don't look back!
Enjoy this change of pace.